The Essential Travis Lane

The Essential
Travis Lane

selected by Shane Neilson

The Porcupine's Quill

Library and Archives Canada Cataloguing in Publication

Lane, M. Travis (Millicent Travis), 1934–
[Poems. Selections]
    The essential Travis Lane / selected by Shane Neilson.

(Essential poets series ; 13)
Poems.
Includes bibliographical references.
ISBN 978-0-88984-388-2 (paperback)

    I. Neilson, Shane, 1975–, editor   II. Title.
III. Series: Essential poets series ; 13

PS8573.A55A6 2015   C811'.54   C2015-905987-9

Published by The Porcupine's Quill, 68 Main Street, PO Box 160,
Erin, Ontario NOB 1TO. http://porcupinesquill.ca

Copyedited by Chandra Wohleber.
Represented in Canada by Canadian Manda.
Trade orders are available from University of Toronto Press.

We acknowledge the support of the Ontario Arts Council and the Canada
Council for the Arts for our publishing program. The financial support of
the Government of Canada through the Canada Book Fund is also
gratefully acknowledged.

Table of Contents

Foreword

I've had tea with Travis Lane at her home in Fredericton many times. During a visit a few years ago, Lane picked up a recent issue of *Poetry* as if it were a limp piece of meat, then theatrically dropped it on the table. 'So much is always in here,' she said with a wink, 'and so rarely is any of it *good*.'

The statement is classic Lane: uncompromising. It also reveals a certain truth about reputations: what's good isn't always where you expect to find it. And Lane is, as it happens, Exhibit A. She's a good poet rarely celebrated. Critics like Guy Hamel have been remarking on the strange disparity since 1980. 'It is important for the sake of her career and of Canadian letters,' he writes, 'that Travis Lane be given a more just recognition than in my judgement she has yet received.'[1] But Lane's career has paralleled that of Canadian letters, existing in a backwater on the world stage.

To be fair, Hamel isn't alone. For Jan Zwicky, Travis is 'a poet of vigorous intelligence and close perception, unafraid to say what she sees.'[2] George Elliott Clarke says, 'Her lines are suffused with a music scored by a feeling intellect, one attuned to nature.'[3] Tim Bowling praises Lane's 'work of high intelligence and assured technique, a combination of the metaphysical and lyrical that derives its power from a careful, visionary analysis of life's quieter moments.'[4]

Though these voices have sway, it is hard to overcome fashion and demographics. First, Lane lives in New Brunswick, not a profitable place to be a poetry networker. Second, she's a woman who found her voice during the seventies and eighties, a time when men had the megaphone. Third, Lane often writes on themes inimical to

---

1. Guy Hamel, review of *Divinations and Shorter Poems 1973–1978*, by M. Travis Lane, *The Fiddlehead* 115 (1977): 97–101.
2. Jan Zwicky, 'How Thought Feels: The Poetics of M. Travis Lane' in *The Book and Its Cover: The Poetry of M. Travis Lane*, ed. Shane Neilson (Victoria: Frog Hollow Press, 2015), 23. Forthcoming.
3. George Elliott Clarke, 'Review of Bartlett and Lane', Halifax *Chronicle Herald*, May 21, 1993.
4. Tim Bowling, 'Brief Reviews — Poetry', *Books in Canada*, no. 24 (1995): 46.

readers, such as politics and spirituality. Her treatment of these subjects is difficult — she does not state things plainly, but rather wrestles with and complicates her themes, constructing her thoughts in a larger framework of meditation on beauty. Fourth, Lane has never applied for a writing grant, meaning that she can't claim to have won a grant and use that as capital when national awards are being given out. After just a few conversations with her, one gets the real and depressing sense that Lane has been overlooked because she didn't aggressively log-roll — it's not in her nature. Fifth, she's not engaged in what can be called the 'Creative Writing–Scene Dominance Strategy'. She taught no creative writing classes, meaning she cultivated no disciples. She never served on the masthead of a magazine or press, although she did plenty of unsung editorial work. Finally, and I weight this factor the most based on the transcendence of her talent, Lane is best in the long-poem mode. Don't just take my word for it: the *Oxford Companion to Canadian Literature* once referred to her as 'the most successful writer of the long poem in the Maritimes.'[5] Because long poems require readerly investment, Lane presents an obstacle up front.

For practical reasons, this slim book isn't the place to remediate that obstacle. I'm happy to report, however, that although Lane's longer poems are among her best achievements, many more great shorter works are hiding in out-of-print volumes. Thus I've primarily excavated Lane's first five books, beginning with *An Inch or So of Garden*, from 1969, and ending with *Reckonings*, from 1988. I end there because the poems in *Solid Things* (1989), her first selected edition with Cormorant, are the ones present-day readers may be most familiar with. Jeanette Lynes' picks from the first half of Lane's career in *The Crisp Day Closing on My Hand* — the second Lane selected, published by Wilfrid Laurier University Press in 2007 — largely duplicate those from the Cormorant title. As a result, Lane's early genius has been relegated to out-of-print books that were never properly recognized in their day. I hasten to add that I leave out poems from Lane's second trade book, *Homecomings*, because it

5. William Toye, *Oxford Companion to Canadian Literature*. Toronto: Oxford University Press, 1983: 515.

consists solely of long poems. It's my hope that Travis' remarkable longer works will one day be triumphantly published in a single volume.

What will you find in *this* volume? Work that is condensed, consonantal and consistent with the current sound techniciary dominating Canadian poetry — *except* that her work espouses far more heart, wisdom and pain than the contemporary obscurity machine can bear. As Lane writes in her poem 'This Being the Case':

> One can not pray for a free thing;
> that a gull land twice on the fire-struck tree —
> for the different voice, the tongue of rocks,
> of a sea spume titans like the motes
> a white gull shakes
> from brightness —

The command of mythic image here is strong. Lane presents a scorched tree, a rock that speaks with divine voice and that classic symbol of freedom, the bird. That the poem starts with the principle that one can't pray to be a captor of free life complicates the list of images — each image is one that cannot be possessed again. That one of these images must free itself from capture by beauty (the gull 'shakes from brightness') adds another layer of complexity.

In the next stanza of the poem, all of humanity is enisled on a 'kiln red island' where 'doom' is 'constant' and, disconcertingly, three voices are made to speak: the sun-voice, the ocean or doom itself! In the third and final stanza, this speaking strands the poem's speaker in place (on a 'sidewalk') and in time ('dumb / as yesterday, tomorrow, and next month'), but also in a poem that amplifies and undercuts its messianic tone depending on the line. God may speak through rocks but it's the poet who's dumb on a sidewalk, considering the eloquent bird.

Lane has documented in poetry a Maritime way of seeing and thinking. Over the years her writing has engaged with faith, nature, feminism, politics and art, but in the past decade she has written incomparably about aging — a universal theme that isn't likely to garner glitzy awards, but one that other senior writers have praised.[6] The poems selected in this volume reflect the aforementioned themes. As a group they keep pace with present-day Canadian poetry but they blow by the contemporary fixation on triviality—Travis writes out her spirit in complex ways, with real technique, using natural symbols to make microcosmal the big, wide world. It should be—and is!—welcoming, invigorating stuff.

—Shane Neilson

6. Nancy Bauer, 'The State of the Art', *Saint John Telegraph-Journal*. Saturday, June 27, 2015: S2.

A Dream for Margaret

Look, there are lights in the lemon trees.
The pale sea quakes
in the lime-belled snares. The orchard floats.
And see — where the lighted ocean flakes,
the long drowned palace quivering
in shadows there.
(Bells nod, chink softly in the foam.)

Where was our scented mansion? There —
where stairs of marble moonlight drift,
the feathered shade
streaks darkness on the foamy steps;
where fireflies come,
slight flakes of meaning touch the air.
The cool lights shaking in the groves
(pale moons of childhood, whispering,)
toll prisoned seas; the meanings fade.
The flecked mermaidens are ourselves,
O Margaret. Pluck not the lime.
Lights in the orchard drown all time.

The Master Builder

Under his long totem the master builder sits.
The crows' wheel crosses overhead, spits rain.
From gloomy feathers silt
falls softly on the cedar bark, discolours
his white blanketing.

He waits the horn of winter when bright gusts
will mount the corners of the sky
and whirl all night the round of art.
His spirit waits the potlatch night,
the pride of all great givings, waits
the horn that summons glory when the camps
will break their separate fires, all stars
come from their lonely darkness bearing gifts,
their torchy glories to the sun.

He waits beside his monument,
his carving flaked, waits, and his fire
so low it barely stirs the moss
to a green flicker. Crows
drop thick forgetfulness and stain
the colours of his tribe.
He waits, waits under dropping time, and feeds
his long endurance, his slow fire, on waiting
for that feast.

Introduction to Caribou City

Let us stand where Murphy's butcher shop
and upstairs dancing was,
and look across the civic spring.
Cattle feed in the woods, and willows grow
in the Potosi ditch where the Fourth of July
parades set fire
those red those sulphur — bands played —
those silver-ores fed the crusher the stamping sky
and lanterns swung, the hydrants gushed,
the gutters swelled in the spatter of smoke
in the bright dust roars and the drum and the fife.
The summer-school boys lost jelly beans down
the board walk, thunder struck the dike,
and the sparks sent off from the Idaho
caught the Constellation's roof,
and the aspens flamed, and the pinwheels spun
like the thirty-eight stars in the school-house flag.

The school-house closed when the winter grew hard.
The original stars have gone back to their lodes.
The marsh reclaims where the butcher shop was.
Those cattle are nosing in the Methodist church.

The Apollonian Whale

From sounding the black valley turns
and thrashes up the bony hills,
the Apollonian whale
breaks water at the peak's crest.
Glaciers streak his mottled sides.
He spouts white music; gusts of wind
roll round him in the swarming sea.
Rose-quartz, white feldspar, glittering pines
break over flukes, frost flanks.
He lolls among the waves of light
and tosses mountains under him.
He swallows sun — great gulps — then turns,
ups tail against the eagles' nest,
thwacks down and splashes warriors out
— his marks strike sky — straight down
his bright back dives into the dark.
He feeds; a giant grubbing black,
he noses green from the black floor.
The cattle crouch in the night groves
and peer at his white gustiness.

Jonah's Song

Under the whale of Earth I hide me,
under the vine, under the root,
under a blanket of turds,
hiding with bulbs,
and I have no words.
And who will spit back Millicent?
I'm safe inside
my Ninevah, my garden green;
it sways, and gleams
like a sea reef—
I have
no words.

Pleasant Things

Yes, they are there of course,
and might be the reason
    to keep on waking
if love didn't find one, always.

There's the day-frond seeking
    the pillow angle,
    the night light making
stars in the shadows, and waters
    tinting the wild snow.

It wouldn't do to know fully
    some things that are done.

But the moon keeps shaking
    the fish lanes; sun
    days are lovely,
    and children speaking
their natural fancy are lovely —

And forests and gardens
and all the green courses
where in the web keeps walking
    the evil man

    Scissoring what
    had not come to its end;
    the spoiler, the procurer,
that from our sons and daughters
    devises the daily show.

    Job at his end
    unreasonably prospered,
   losing the truth of his mortal horror;
'What,' says the Lord from his iron hearses
   to ignorant weak and the sick in mercy
   'Can poor I do Who can only Know?'

This Being the Case

One can not pray for a free thing;
that a gull land twice on the fire-struck tree —
for the different voice, the tongue of rocks,
of a sea spume titans like the motes
a white gull shakes
from brightness —

that more than once only the sun-voice,
the ocean wrapped in a yellow stare,
or, out of the kiln red island,
doom constant — speak —

Free goes the gull, in many tongues ascending,
and leaves me sidewalk foolish, dumb
as yesterday, tomorrow, and next month —
a pole stuck in the ground, dry buoy —
with no such thing
as tongue.

Spring Break-up

Like a ruined leaf a bird's bones hang
upside down in the night wind,
a star in the beak. They claim
the night and sun as one, a winter
health. The river bed's dry rock
where door-light pounds,
mallet-blank on the skinned, white sun.

My winter-time keeps healthy,
holds itself, puts nothing forward —
a house canned smug in country cold
in plastic skirts, its door nailed shut,
stiff as a skate, all surface. Here
my dry poles mark the highway edge,
paved river, and forget that lurks
beneath our jangling, market noise
the wild, invisible gold eye —
the emerald, the watery ghost.

The little lives that flowers have —
in grass, this people, stinking up
in charnel paths spring-times.

Stronger than roots the pulled land bleeds
where they dug us up going nowhere
faster than words have tongues.
Soot dries the bud where green hands held
a candle shine: a little eye
in the grass blown out
like a sun to seed....

George Fox in his meadow saw his way
to light the London wise and break
the foot-thick shining roads
to drink of, seeing yonder gate.
In truck-loads to the truck-land mind,

sacked wives and kids with greasy eyes
wallow to Ives; the people is —
grass, is grass, like asses' ears,
like river reeds, the golden touch …
but Fox went on in the gentle way,
lighting the candle, the basket shine.

God's gander. What the angel said:
go buy a digging stick, or spin.
In Adam's plot. Repent, repent,
the echoes delve. I file away
a carbon conscience unrepaid.
The drawer glides easy on its rings,
plastic and sweet in the morning red.

'Little good has my health been to others,'
said Frost, grown old; the Quaker Fox
with less of night still wondered too —
What good to touch soul-splattered men
or mark the truck-land charm that writes
child's blood on doors: 'Go easy by,
sweet bomber, brother, dinosaur —'
to shame our brunt material.

What good? Now the enormous noise
of sunlight gathers up; I skate
on surfaces; my health
is door closed, winter-time. Put out,
Friend, put it out, that light —

For Fox's leather-britched ghost
reproaches, meek as fish-faint shades
in river ice; he cracks the roads,
is dangerous. Go look, he says,
in the back yard. For out of death,
spring puts again
its usual, tiny lights.

The Hayman

The hayman's feet, like brown trout,
hide in the stones. What day commands
heaps on his head. A summer's heat
dims all: a cupped circumference
mid-day, a moon in brass.
But long hills lie within him,
sea-fogs inwardly, and pines,
translating the god winds,
shadow his sleeping thoughts.

The Statue

Phaedrus, trans. Bowra

'The eyes of a living man, but wonderfully silent' —
The charioteer of grace directs
the unseen horses of the veins,
driving the solar intellect — And still we cross
the noon's distinct meridian, living, awake,
but wonderfully silent....

Wheels in the air evolve no words — discreet, a poetry
of pulse-beat only and the weight of wings, heart tumult —
and the noon's glare sliding — to the red,
sun-darkening — sea....

'The eyes of a living man' — but art
is wonderfully silent: and still we cross
wings in the air succeeding selves and our selves, Ezekiel;
with only the art receding — and the sun's —
cart....

Cede self, soul, and the wing-beat, and the wheels in the air.
For strive, and the art strives stronger, silent,
over the sea's churn,
silent....

More living than I are the eyes of grace
that wonderfully silent — revolving —
that wonderfully silent —
stare....

Plain Stars

'Come un bel dí di Maggio'

Plain stars in an unheated night
beyond this plain slant out
their temporal fartherings, fine farers;
like the summer's yachts
they dot this lined circumference,
each sphering in a crocus light
to balanced towers,
committed to this season's flight
beyond the cyclones of despair
to the eternal circumstance.

If from this cold a lonely monster yearns
against the Gold Pavilion that is ours,
the phoenix for our ashes; if he burns
pavilion, towers, yachts — and low
Okigbo lies with Chénier in our dust,
those stars still slant —

The Song of Lot's Wife

Out of the living rock I fashioned drink:
out of the rock
that followed me, the convolute,
lipped, whorled rock, ear stone, that sang
the ocean to the falls,
that shouldering nocturnal steams
from the ice-hunkered rivers, dragon raked,
lumped up in leaden gully streaks,
inscribed brief names in briny coals,
sea-licked, ephemeral, a drink.
This is the rock that singing stands,
the Sion in the wilderness,
earth's dark, corroding tune.

i.

The eagles map on Chamcook's side
the generations' names.
The branded rock whets hunters' knives
with facelessness. I watched
the deer come down in fall,
like coals to fire; the porcupine
records the bones. Good hunting
by the picnic glass the buggies broke
Dominion Day, a century ago, but death
has no dominion.
We drink this cup once only;
then the season's closed.

ii.

The shotgun's temporary marks
like airplane shadows spot the hill:
it is no hawk that circles there—
Lie flat. The hunter's cap's
a monument. They stalk each other,
fawn and doe. And here,
the child lost in the bush
is gutted with a rabbit knife—
a picnic for the veterans,
Remembrance Day.
The Lord provides.

iii.

What is the shadow on the rock?
A bird's crossed wings, a diving drone…?
This tide-crouched rock's
a look-out tower. Where I stand,
on every side the white-streaked
salt blocks of the towns
from sea to sea cry out dominion,
death. The fire bells ring.
Marked children to this hill return
to write themselves. On Moses' rock
the wild deer browse.
Two thirds of death
lies hidden, berg stone
in the grass.
I fish this rock.

iv.

The cut rock sings
that follows me
of death, dominion, Sion....
Ash to ash. The written name
is worm flesh, bud of Moses' pond,
the temporary; he who runs
can read.
Lot's wife turned back.
One stone she is
with the grief of God,
singing a song
of Sion.

v.

By the salt lick, deer
come down to drink,
the hart from the hill.
From grief I drank.
All soils distill
this water.

What Moves Is Held

Sky-towed, the starry barges heave
at tide ropes in predicted arcs,
like plankton drift circuitous;

Each plotted speck
flecked off the constant refuse heap
rises and falls divinely stirred
to ebb in grace constraintly fluxed:

What moves is held.

The hair that slipped from Jonah's beard
treks through the stars
the protein predicates of mass;

Iron-tongued, lodestone compelled,
the meteor journalists sing on the hills
a poetry pre-spun;

Nor speech nor language but the sound
goes out into all nations compassed by
the clouds of moving witnesses,
the condetermined names.

For each
has news, a grace, a logic
to pronounce. I speak
as must this handiwork:

What moves is held.

At Night Up Here the Road Is Different

At night up here the road is different,
for then the black-green angels of the woods
sidle like fish in the glassy air at the brown
night's edge. The trucker's nap; Orion's sign,
the hunter's blaze, sparkles on darkened behemoths.
Along this road five hundred miles of trees
scrape night-time skies engraving verse
in black-fly glyphics like the smokes put out
two years ago in King's, or like the ghosts
the ice received, opening up last winter,
the trappers trapped, like things you see
only when you're up here and late enough.

The sky's miasma yellow now: a miner's dawn
all night, scum paradise. For this each night
the northern trucker wakes, repills, and takes
the road beside the tracks flat out, flat on,
his carbon trail fringing the highway's wings
like prayers, or bills on a spindle, or like fumes
from shallow ponds that mount the angels'
bristle backs spring mornings burning water or
again like the jet message settling sky
over the trees' ears thicker, and for this,
dead angels carry trucks piggyback, and lumber-flats.

The trucker makes you understand. Up here
angelic speech makes news: fish gutted catacombs
of spruce, jack-pine, and stunted fir go to the pot,
the sulphur stew, that smells from here like gospel airs —
and fuel the trucks, the lily fields, and the jet
vapor tracks above the shuttered hunter's camp,
nailed, for the winter, shut.

For Derek Walcott

Like you, we have no home. This hospital of leaves,
winds rattling in the absences of speech
between your steaming ocean and our fogs
is, like our dingy sorrow, well to grief.
For all that rigorous anger is the vogue
you could not cut us, cousin, from your blood,
blood kin, for all the tyrannies of ghosts,
evil endured, enduring, and maintained.
And yet the bloody footprints on the beach
spoke like a rose our languages. We reach
the same familiar knowledge: not alone,
but sharing this, the central gulf of pain.
Poet of our passaging, in you, we are 'half-home'.

Mirrorings

The girls have all drowned in her mirror;
one after one in the water
that closes smooth as steel
each morning dying after them.

Now floats their image:
wind-soiled swan that floats
this greasy river with the scows,
the gray gulls beating over head.

The sun-set streaks the narrows;
swan becomes
a candle in the river's shift:
the image, flame in a paper skiff,
from the smooth park pond has slid
under the dark, curved highway bridge,
into the river's murk.

Between glass sky and river glides
the gnat-brief coracle of light,
the protean immediate, the fire-swan
drifts the mirror down
beyond this civic medium.

Cold morning in the marshes brings
a poetry of snow: salt feathers,
melting reeds — the swans of mist
go up into the sun til noon;
they drown in air, faint ladies, whose
transparent dyings haze the glass.
The river holds the image up,
dispersing it. Tide turns.

Beyond the falls the whirlpools catch
and spin the shape; it slides
under the evening cool as flies
on the speck-breasted river glass —
a flicker where the mirror drains
the dimming skies collecting light
into the darkness, shining.

Giants hang over the water,
and under it lurk;
drowned eyes in the mirror:
sea-walls, cod drift, and mewling stars —
The cold rock hammers on the bay;
the fire ship darkens in the salt, slides out
upon its darkening,

Until the spangled sea itself
responds in phosphorus and strikes
match flames from insect reckonings
to smallest touch angelic,
equatorial.

And in that equal mirror breaks
the single image to all suns,
all daughters million moted, shined,
in one sea drowned, and living,
in one retrieving
flame.

I've Been to My Sweetheart's

My love's an IBM machine, sitting all risks.
Where have you been, my Absalom?
Spindled, split on the daily psalm.
My hymn book broke and the beans fell out,
all spickled and speckled, in hedges and ditches —
Make my bed soon.

The console's on; compute. What average
lies waste and desolate? Deliver
in the time of trial: tick, tick.

Bend, fold, mutilate, stick through —
Sebastian, where the arrows shine
each marks a nick on Peter's card:
tick, tick. For every stone,
lay one aside.

As I stood on the road on the way home,
civil enough, a sojourner in waste,
stones and propriety came to my hand —
and my eyes were burned.

There's a thorn in my flesh, tick, tick,
marking the wounds, in hands, in feet,
in the side where the little cards go in:

Who spilled the beans?
I've been to my sweetheart's. Make my bed.
For my eyes have seen.

The Grindstone

The grindstone unattached,
       listless,
         solidifies
     all atmosphere:
    'Love I am not and not death.
     I am no wheel.

    Too factual,
    I am no use.
    I sharpen nothing.
     Still,
  I blunt all winds.

    In me
  the actual forgets
     itself
  in actual. I sit
beyond all turning. Am
      Not and my not:
    the wheel.'

Astronomical

The night is a pond in a needle's eye:
    Plink! and a frog or a sputnik flares
    under the needle; the spheroids flail
    polar tad-tailed in their spindling course.
        Galactic diatoms obscure
        love's year perennial: minnow flash
        under the milk
        dark.

The night is a gate in a needle's eye:
    the dance wheels round; in a shuttler's bend
    Time weaves and darts her golden thread;
    looping unseen, she spins the pond
        the beaded Hippocrene where suns,
        fish-flies in the sky-sein,
        strain at knots of love incarnate;
        swallow gnats.

The night's opaque; is a looking glass.
Could a frog or a fish or a wise man pass
this gate with Alexandrine stroke?
    With Venus at hand and Love in the bush
    around spins the mote in the dusty road,
        in the minnow path, in the milk dark,
        in the gate of night, still looking,
        in the skim, decanted
        cold.

The Burning Bush

Barberry burns and strong fir leaps
like tongues, like languages; each leaf
shrivels in words; the forest makes
a furnace-mouth where martyrs break,
drop flesh, drop green, all body sweets,
blessed now with grace too bright, too brief
to bear. The ghost enburdens, wears
election and assumption; here's
no dove descending in a hush
but glory in a burning bush;
snake-headed, many tongued,
it sings, it flowers; but never fruit
will gather from this serpent's soot.

I have walked past a quiet place:
grace, the blessing; grass, the grace;
the rich anonymous replace
past grandeurs. Here and there a trace:
charred standards, bone-house scraping yet,
unhuddled roots against the rock —
these flew high flags, withstood storm's shock,
held birds, shook golden pollen down,
and fruited fully. Toppled down.
Who names the nations underground?
I have not seen the grace that charred,
but only jackstraw forests, marred.

Walk here in grass and mourn the shock
that splintered fire-crowns from the rock.
This meadow peace is not so brief;

The quiet waters dew the leaf and grass
obliviates all grief.
But nothing is so quiet grown
that fire is ever known unknown.
'Look here,' the bitter night appeals,
the forests burning in its wheels.
I have not seen but I have seen.
Each star exhausts
the pentecosts.

Spring Sours

Where the stained spring sours by the chemical marsh,
neither orchis nor eagle; and salmon fail —
a meaningless fish — where the sprayed spruce stand —
rolled in the soot-mist the old myths
dwindle into the paper mills —
But there's a bird in the lilac bush,
wan, and palely loitering —
by six sick elms, and turf-o-green.
And there's a pigeon on the park bench!
And a dandelion —
like an old religion: for children only,
and the low in mind.

But It IS Hard

But it IS hard
when who knows why —

                  fell —

and for each man different —

Vulgar your ways. Indifferent —
the finite winds,
and the sloughing off —

but ever a little in tender heat
the sea-blown inquiry of dust
blossoms to man —

can a jump of my soul —

                  grab at —

to be one syllable?

          Ah.   Yes.

A Stone from Fundy

You, dear, and I,
and the tide shall flow
through the Fundy gate
with the bladder-wrack.
On Hopewell's strand
the moon shape's still
what it always is.
I scrawl
moon shapes in quartz,
in shale — long oblongs,
crack
eccentric fish-lines in pale slate
(I and the tide together).
Can only the moon
with her white, salt gaze
myopic with steam, with bladder-wrack,
decipher? The soft waves suck.
The days
slip by. Hold out your hand.
Here
is a small
stone.

Walking Under the Nebulae

From my thumb in the hole in my pocket, warm,
to the Crab or the edge of Snickers' dust,
is a cold hole flocked with gossamer,
goose-quill electrons, spiral snails
of geologic colloids, gas (fern spores
for blind astronomers) —
                              less
than the field mouse in the hedge
curled in his womb position like a leaf.

Walking under the nebulae, I want to breathe
with a monster breath, to have that soreness
in my paws, each step the consequential fate
keeping entire me. But on me's only
the golden vault, sky's bubble upon me,
one eye in a wilder vastness that,
myopic mouse in a lost hole, me,
life, the essential, is —
                              too small
to hold it.

The Grand Mirrors at Versailles

In the hall of grand mirrors the dusky glass
is blue as if bruised, as if the dead's blue
unreflecting eyes looked out and mirrored woods,
grey, empty fields, the motionless canals.
This ballroom's like a clearing in the woods:
the chandeliers drip like wet leaves;
rich walls and watery curtains frame
the trees' drenched velvets, muddy paths, and,
indoors and out, white statues with their blank
primeval gaze.
                    It's Veterans' Day.

Mustered along the stable yard's
hoof-bruising cobbles — black and orange —
the regimental standards flare. Their green
king waves toward the Grand Parade from his brass
horse. He likes a sense of history:
to gild blue eyes like mirrors, fill
his yards with music, banners, guns —
la gloire....

                    The sheds are closed.
All buttoned up alike: the swords, the flags,
the crimson reins, and the gilded sleds
for the Grand Canal — the tortoise with its agate eyes,
bear-headed silks and palm-treed runners, gilt —
and the great bronze tank, Bonaparte's
state carriage tonned by blinded angels with mute horns
and leaden flowers like the wreaths
on the little graves of soldiers, cooks, yard-boys
who bruised in the long, grey fields
for the eyes in the grand, blue mirrors.

Here where Marie's brown ditch reflects
only the sky, in the green furred woods
the loud unseeable wild birds sing their
petite eternity, the same they sang
when Louis tried his fountains — frogs who showed
the courtiers what they were, stone men, stone frogs,
stone deities, and Neptune freezing in his pond —
the same they sang when our blue troops
stone-hearted drained from watery fields
their cousins; but the birds forget. Deaf mirrors show
only our wavery human shapes — mute as the brown ditch flow.

Matins

for Quasimodo

The cock in its winter fortress crows
to ice-defeated crevices, inaudible,
except to you, half-sunken in a silence of your own.
No actual moon; the night is split in half.
An eggy dawn
has ringed the smoky turret with its light —
pieta of the trans-
autumnal marys of the world, what was,
grown deaf, in landscapes of the heart.

Last Picnic

for my grandmother

A long concourse of light,
a hot pure breadth and fullness sweeps
rolling into the grey hills west
of this light's edge. The land
leans in the wind, flesh-coloured,
the furred seed tassels rippling.

From Wildcat's ridge the grasslands stretch
towards the bouldered hills, cottonwood
crouched in their orange arroyos —
a picnic view: to see the sun
kindle the distant snow-peaks as it falls.

The fire smudge centres us. Below
the late day lingers in the scrub
thickening shades to buffalo,
ghosts of the old adventurers.
From here a thread road lines the valley depths,
leads to the 'mad man's castle', some say,
'eagle's nest', miniature, stone among stone,
to us, from our eye eyrie.

Twilight billows like a fog
around us on our separate liths
like crones, the weird Ward women, so alike
same voice, same face, same distances.

Then, louring from the west, the cloud
that lion-tawny crept towards us,
that jelled the coyote's yip to glass,
divided us — not then,
but in my memory then —

as absolute as that clear wall
the bare stars have beyond our bloom
eye-burning, honeyless, whose creak
pilots the empty passages —

It was as if one spirit leaped —
as a bird flings up from the pine mast tip
and spurs out on the peach fire of the west
buoying its wings on upper winds
we only know of by its flight,
leaning in towards the mountains, sure —

as an ash wheels into the greying sky
from one doused picnic campfire,
and is gone.

That Eye

Like sheep in the front of a ferry or
at first, so herded together they seemed,
those frowsled, burr-entangled men —
til one looked back.
                              Like a wolverine's
that yellow eye — that sneering from the shore
slid from the cliffs and the hound's slick tooth —
between the wrack-encrusted rocks
moved on the waters — no voice — no name —
rust staining the deck and the tow-rope chains —
an eye — a man's — like a livid flame.

Colonial

Our little bells ring steadily;
beyond them drones
the deaf Atlantic sponging us,
dot on a dull map, from our sight.
A white mist surges from our dreams
and blocks our harbours,
tamps us down, conceived
in exile, nothingness.

We have our meanings in the clay.
Across it the ground juniper
sends its long fingers, frost
cracking the gravestones, antlers
rotting among the epitaphs —
Nothing is here. But there —
where that far freighter makes its slow
unyielding passage to the sky
climbing as out of a teapot boil
into the lucent calcimine,
there, there, our treasure is —

for home is a place we've never been.
We would not be home in it were we there.

Raven

after an image of Susan Musgrave's

Holding your own at the seaside
you have eyes
to hold the visible in lines and draw
your sustenance from stone and salt,
minding the river.

'Incredibly arcane' the visible image,
in this case
a grey beach struck by a white sea,
wind coming heavy.

The ravens stand
like totems on it, like black chess.
Clams wink at the river's entering.

She said, 'They sewed the river up
when it gashed dry
with dogs' eyes, sewed it up again.'

The artery feeds
a giant's heart.

The ravens play
the visible, heroes of fable,

immortal game,
their motto running the river's course:

'Never withdraw.'

The Healed Child

Death kept his tendril fondling
the baby's head, stitched up
and blonding like the spring.
And though she flowers all the same
among the bright girls' birchen grove,
his stencil tattooed on her skin
cries 'Mine. Mine.'
                          Although Proserpine
came back, the red seed in her skull,
and flowered to a golden age
tucking her parents down at last
whose nightly candles burned for her
like leaves on the mantled water,
like wet prayers, their voices
sighing from the grass, still weep
'Come back. Come back.'

The Anodyne

The wash of time, drowsy as ever,
where the combers narrow our clinging chores
like an old surf buried in dreaming,
like an airplane droning, receding,
smooths into watery countries
our dozy hours.

A child sparks up; ash in the wind.
Dark angels tore
our kindled blossoms.
Night winds drunk them; better so.
The sleeper yearns for sleep;
to lose
into watery countries
the irretrievable lost.

Bride in the Fish Market

The little bride pelted with March rain
runs down through the fish market, scales
like confetti upon the wet stones,
holds on to her brother, past shelves
of slabbed oysters, of black-furred sea-urchins,
red snappers, spilled pails
of chicken guts, yellow claws ...
                                Looming ahead,
its dirty grey windows half-open, Eustache,
St. Eustache of Les Halles,
heaves at its moorings, a trawler at dock.
The jackhammer drilling beside its piles
marries bride after bride, Pigeon, the mariner,
Fidgeting flits from pillar to speaker.
The scrub pail waits by the altar rail
for the work to go on.
          The great stone belly is full of light,
its hold lace-vaulted with sagging nets
and visible fish, if the saints are fish —
cod, mackerel, squid in the cornices,
tourists in wet boots, scallop shells —
all Saturday morning again and again —
and the bridegroom comes ...

Ready to Sleep

I rest and the ways weave by me —
      ready to run, if I must run,
      ready to sleep, if I may sleep.
            (Fish under, and great hawk over.)

Begin from Sunyata's corona and sleep:
      Under the cove the plastic card
      unlocks your conscience, the red scar child —
            (Is it your dreaming I trample on?)

From the deep brook moose lifts his dripping head,
looks at me: animal consciousness.
      Less of it asked.

But the gold corona slips over,
      the prayer shawl singing the natural debt,
      forgiveness, nature's removal,
      new grass under the rim of light.

Your sleep may safely graze,
      muzzle in water, in shadow shapes,
      the spent ships leaning on black tides —

      where only the petal slips soft to the sea —
            (Fish under, and great hawk over.)

Sleeping Children

Night's children lulled by the highway's din
open their stony fists to flowers;
the stuttering street-light angels them
with sleep; the blue moths of their lids
quiver alive like a lake's dreams
where all of the day hangs upside-down,
drowningly rainbowed.

Need

Need is a spare island: a beach
rubbed clear of diamonds,
a moon-pronged antler,
a white tree trunk
scoured by the urgencies of sand —

as if plain weather could redeem
our cankers, drain
our inward autumns!

                    Time,
(oh boats, oh voyageurs)
absorbing breast of water, take
your paddlers like apprentices
and ease us out of memory to rest —
excursion on the instant of your lap
rolled round in time's abstraction,
sleep —

            and you will dream us as we were,
childlike and rowing in your sea
hung round with stars and majesties,
the intimate, tender netherlands
from which our fountains leap.

The Stars This Evening

The stars this evening were always there.
I could not call a cloud to pass
among them, varying their pace,
but in the ocean under them I dip my hand.
And where the ripples runnel, phosphor flakes
make diatomic galaxies, insect gleams
like fireflies these soft summers on the lawn.

Those little lights, like star lights,
are still there. It needs my hand
to bring their natural glory to your sight,
if not my hand — the surf,
a late fish leaping for pure joy —
See how the darkness pummels into flame?

The poem moves in darkness,
and makes light.

'Only Connect'

A lavish hand for little us, God's —
or perhaps that hydrogen
that trims the mind's circumference,
lavish, and always distanter.
So close at home
we feel the waning of the heart.
The edges of the universe, the Word,
retire. The friends die off.
The child sets out on labyrinths.
Goodbye. Goodbye.
What hand can reach out towards us from that dark?

But do we want a motion from the dead?
A hand that rises from the sea,
shakes, and, its fingers numbing,
fails.
        It slips against our gunnels, sinks.
The boat bobs on the inky waves.
I grab the oars. They thump and rap,
a vulgar spirit ouija-ing, not real,
not real. We all escape, grow separate.

More room, more room, the March Hare cried,
space head.   .

Corduroy

Porthos, you should be with me in this hour.
My facing snagged, revealed my shabby corduroy,
guilt-crimpled like a candy's foil.
What did we read those damn books for?

For just your glint of tinsel, yes,
your Atlas strength.
Old fatty, with your burlap touch
you kept the tune. Our candied life,
weighted with lies, will smother us.

The dog star barks,
holding the other stars at bay.
They drop their glittering fakeries,
indifferent, reveal
the shoddy cavern as it sags.
'Machines,' he cried. 'Too heavy,' and his heart
broke then. The stars lost sight.

He was their eyes.

Any Day Now

Spring fattens the buds on the ice-bent trees,
humours a little. Three blocks away
a dog barks. This specific day
resembles a little the any day —
any day now — an illness, fire,
an error in the clouds. Serene
among the offices a death
stalks like a kitten. A twitch,
a wriggle in the leaves — poof — out —
so casual, that indolent
cuff. The whole stays whole.
The day seals round the incident
like a yeast rising loaf.

Your Other Word

Against the flowing whiteness of Your light
I feel the breathing spaces of my kin,
those cricket worlds of thin skies
farther than words can travel to —

but this word comes, Your other word,
our old familiar consciousness
dusting the dark with human pain,
the traveller sown by the high hill.

What is the word but the change in the surf,
or the salt that dries on the swimmer's lips —
says out of the swimming, *freedom*,
and out of the freedom, *pain* —

Road Ending

At the end of the road a hunter's hut
boarded all summer, the fraying bush
backing against it, a ragged fringe
of beggar's ticks, rust tassels, thorns,
and boulders pushed to the water's edge
where the graders turned.
There was no one home.

And no one in the water. Overhead
the white threads spidered from a jet
drifted across where the evening star
was not yet shining.

What were the words I could not use,
the thoughts I could not think to say?
The white lake shook in the early dusk.

Something was lost we were waiting for,
summer, perhaps, or snow.

About Travis Lane

Millicent Elizabeth Travis Lane was born in San Antonio, Texas, on September 23, 1934. As the daughter of Army/Air Force Colonel William Livingston Travis (1908–1998) and Elsie Ward Travis (1913–2010), she travelled around much of the United States during her early life due to her father's military postings.

She entered Vassar University in 1952 and earned her B.A. in 1956, also editing and publishing in the *Vassar Review*. Her thesis, *The Fences of Robert Frost: The Changes in His Ways of Approaching Philosophical Problems*, was awarded an M.A. in 1957 by Cornell. After the thesis was expanded into *Agnosticism as Technique: The Poetry of Robert Frost*, Lane was awarded a Ph.D. in 1967.

In 1960 she moved to Fredericton with Dr. Lauriat (Larry) Lane Jr., her husband, and Hannah, her one-year-old daughter. The family moved north because Dr. Lane took a job with the Department of English at the University of New Brunswick. In a 'What Happened When He Went to the Store for Bread' moment, Larry, a nature lover, had decided to take the job because (1) he was delighted that a fox darted across the Fredericton Airport runway as his plane touched down, and (2) the political climate in Canada was more temperate than in red-scared America, as evidenced during the conclusion to his interview with the university president, when Dr. McKay said, 'Now I have to go and play tennis with the campus communist!'

Lane raised Hannah and her son, Lauriat Lane III, while working as Honorary Research Associate for the Department of English. She holds that position to the present day. She became a Canadian citizen in 1973. She has published fifteen books of poetry and has also served as an astute reviewer of poetry for the *Fiddlehead* and other Canadian periodicals for almost fifty years. Along the way she has won the Atlantic Poetry Prize, the Pat Lowther Memorial Award and the Banff Centre Bliss Carman Poetry Award. She is a member of the Raging Grannies and Voice of Women for Peace. She is a founding member as well as Honorary President of the Writers' Federation of New Brunswick. She is a Life Member of the League of Canadian Poets, participating vociferously in its Feminist Caucus.

Travis Lane continues to write poems and reviews. Her latest book, *Crossover*, was published by Cormorant this year.

Selected Bibliography

An Inch or So of Garden. New Brunswick Chapbook No. 6, 1969.

Poems 1968–1972. Fredericton: Fiddlehead Poetry Books, 1973.

Homecomings: Narrative Poems. Fredericton: Fiddlehead Poetry Books, 1977.

Divinations and Shorter Poems 1973–1978. Fredericton: Fiddlehead Poetry Books, 1980.

Reckonings: Poems 1979–1985. Fredericton: Goose Lane Editions, 1985.

Solid Things: Poems New and Selected. Dunvegan, ON: Cormorant, 1989.

Temporary Shelter: Poems 1986–1990. Fredericton: Goose Lane Editions, 1993.

Night Physics. London, ON: Brick Books, 1994.

Keeping Afloat. Toronto: Guernica, 2001.

Touch Earth. Toronto: Guernica, 2006.

The Crisp Day Closing on My Hand: The Poetry of M. Travis Lane. Jeannette Lynes, ed. Waterloo: Wilfrid Laurier University Press, 2007.

The All-Nighter's Radio. Toronto: Guernica, 2010.

The Book of Widows. Victoria: Frog Hollow Press, 2010.

Ash Steps. Markham: Cormorant, 2012.

Crossover. Markham: Cormorant, 2015.